Therapy Has Gone to the Dogs

Gone to the Dogs

The Therapist's Guide to

Animal Assisted Therapy

by Susan Kelsey, MFT, RPT-S

TABLE OF CONTENTS

INTRODUCTION

I am a Marriage and Family Therapist in private practice, and my practice is dedicated solely to the treatment of children and adolescents and their families. Recently I gave presentations at several psychotherapy conferences in California on Animal Assisted Therapy. Part of my presentation included showing video interviews with my young clients explaining what it meant to them to work with my therapy dog, "Scamp." Even children who didn't tend to interface with the dog very much during their sessions used phrases such as "He understands how I feel" and "I was so scared to go to therapy until I saw Scamp was there." In many cases I didn't fully realize how important the presence of the dog was to these children until I did these interviews.

Ten years ago when I decided to include a dog in my therapy practice there was little information for therapists on the legal, ethical, or practical implications of including an animal in a psychotherapy practice. Since that time I have learned quite a bit – primarily from my own intuitions, experience, and research into the literature on animals and therapy. This handbook is presented as a general guide for therapists who are considering adding an animal to their practice. I hope to help therapists take a realistic look at whether this might be a viable option for them. It is by no means an endorsement for using an animal in your practice. There are many things to consider, and it is certainly not an option for everyone.

Since I work solely with children and adolescents, much of the information presented here is focused on working with children. However most concepts can be applied to working with adults as well. In addition, my experience has been with using a dog in my practice, but other animals (such as cats, rabbits, birds, etc.) can be considered. If you wish to use an animal other than a dog, you will need to find a therapy animal screening group that can test and certify your specific animal.

This handbook is by no means intended to be all inclusive in its content regarding Animal Assisted Therapy and should not be viewed as the information you will need to consider yourself trained in Animal Assisted Therapy. You will need special training which is provided by various groups designed for this purpose. The legal and ethical issues I present here are also not intended to be all inclusive. I have presented a sampling of considerations in these areas, and you will need to do your own research on these issues in the state in which you are licensed to practice psychotherapy.

I hope to introduce you to the practice of Animal Assisted Therapy, share some of the research on the subject, consider some of the legal, ethical, and practical issues related to this practice, and share ways I have used this technique in my practice.

"There is no psychiatrist in the world like a puppy licking your face."

Ben Williams

WHAT IS ANIMAL ASSISTED THERAPY?

The Pet Partners (formerly called Delta Society) defines Animal Assisted Therapy as the use of an animal as either a treatment by itself or an addition to an existing treatment, such as psychotherapy. They explain that Animal Assisted Therapy is not a style of therapy, however. This approach uses an animal as a tool while operating from the therapist's principle foundational method. Animal Assisted Therapy is a goal-directed intervention in which an animal is a primary element of the treatment process (Delta Society, 2009). Barker & Dawson (1998) describe Animal Assisted Therapy as an interaction between patients and a trained animal and human handler with a therapeutic objective.

You may be familiar with animals who, along with trained handlers, visit rest homes or hospitals. These animals are usually performing "Animal Assisted Activities", not Animal Assisted Therapy. Animal Assisted Activities are activities that involve animals visiting people and provide opportunities of motivational, educational, and/or recreational benefits to enhance the quality of life. Animal Assisted Activities are delivered in a variety of environments by a specially trained professional, paraprofessional, and/or volunteer in association with animals that meet specific criteria (Delta Society).

Animal Assisted Activities differ from Animal Assisted Therapy in several other specific ways. First, where detailed notes are required in Animal Assisted Therapy, they are not required for Animal Assisted Activities. Animal Assisted Activities do not require specific treatment goals like Animal Assisted Therapy, and Animal Assisted Activities visits tend to be spontaneous and may only last a few minutes.

In addition, where Animal Assisted Activities may be delivered by a volunteer, such as a volunteer handler who along with their trained animal visit residents of a nursing home, Animal Assisted Therapy is delivered by a professional in the provision of therapeutic services.

In California where I am licensed as a psychotherapist it appears that Animal Assisted Activities are far more regulated than Animal Assisted Therapy. To be able to go to a hospital or rest home with your animal you are required to have training and your animal is required to have passed a screening test. Not so it seems with animals used in therapy practices.

There appears to be little or no regulation or requirements for this practice, and many therapists are bringing their untrained animal to work. I'd like to see this change for the safety of all.

"Petting, scratching, and cuddling a dog could be as soothing to the mind and heart as deep meditation and almost as good for the soul as prayer"

Dean Koontz, *False Memory*

HISTORY AND RESEARCH

American psychiatrist Boris Levinson, who is considered the father of animal-assisted therapy, summarized the importance that animals could have in people's lives in several articles published in the 1960's and 1970's. Levinson believed that an emotional relationship with an animal is in itself a physiological intervention comparable to a drug.

Although these certainly do not represent all that are out there, I found several research articles on using an animal in psychotherapy or related topics. A groundbreaking study in 1980 showed that "pet owners had lower blood pressure and triglyceride levels than did non-pet owners" (Barker & Dawson, 1998, p. 797). Rieichert (1994) paired the use of play and Animal Assisted Therapy in a group treatment model for sexually abused girls aged 9-13. She reports that "throughout the session the therapy dog is present. Sometimes children hold the pet in order to ease tension, reflect anxiety, or for support. Some of the children decide to whisper the story of their sexual abuse in the ear of the dog instead of the other group members, and the children often looked to the dog for emotional support." It has also been found that animals have a "de-arousing effect" on humans & provide people with stress-reducing or stress-buffering social support (Serpell, 2000, p. 15). Parshall (2003) researched the use of animals in mental health settings and examined clinical, treatment, legal, ethical, and cultural issues. Kovacs (2004) did a pilot study on animal-assisted therapy for middle-aged schizophrenic patients living in a social institution. Every area assessed by Kovacs had changed positively, with significant changes in domestic and health activities. He believed Animal Assisted Therapy had a positive impact. The severely impaired patients formed a strong bond with the dog. Prothmann et al. (2006) investigated possible influences of Animal Assisted Therapy on the state of mind of children and adolescents who had undergone inpatient psychiatric treatment. Following five individual therapeutic sessions with a therapy dog, compared to the control group, the treatment group demonstrated increased alertness, attention, openness and desire for social contact, perception of healthy and vital factors, and participants appeared psychologically more well-balanced. These effects appeared stronger the worse the individual felt before the contact with the dog. Lange, Cox et al (2007) examined the inclusion of an animal in group counseling with adolescents in an anger management group, and concluded that some of the benefits included calming effects, humor relief, safety in disclosing, experiences of empathy, and motivation for attending sessions. Pichotand Coulter (2007) introduced Animal Assisted solutions-focused, brief therapy. Minatrea & Wesley (2008) combined Animal Assisted Therapy and Reality Therapy (RT) as a method to facilitate a positive therapeutic relationship. Sockalingam, Li, et al (2008) did a clinical case study that they believed demonstrated the effectiveness of Animal Assisted Therapy in the psychiatric rehabilitation of an assault victim with a concurrent mood disorder. The case highlighted the use of Animal Assisted Therapy with an antidepressant and mood stabilizer in a patient with Bipolar I and atypical depression. The goal of these concerted efforts was sustained improvement in the patient's level of functioning. They did not notice any negative effects of utilizing a therapy dog in these hospital settings, and both the patients and the families asked for the dog to return and participated regularly in the therapy, with no drop-outs. F. Walsh (2009) examined the role of pets in family systems and family therapy, and concluded that including companion animals as valuable resources in systemic assessments and interventions can inform and enrich therapeutic work with couples and families. R. Jasperson (2010) looked at matching Animal Assisted Therapy techniques and interventions with counseling theories. Another case example from a pilot program published by R. Jasperson (2010) showed the use of animal-assisted therapy with female inmates with mental illness. Jasperson found that the Animal Assisted Therapy intervention was well received by group members, the mental health workers, and the Department of Corrections administration. Anecdotally, the group's facilitator, participants, and their clinicians reported positive outcomes.

"A dog is the only thing on earth that will love you more than he loves himself."

Josh Billings

Not all articles I encountered regarding the use of animals in therapy were positive, however. The Los Angeles Times (July 18, 2011) published an article called "Therapy dogs make the rounds in more healthcare settings" where they tout the proposed benefits of using a therapy animal, but questioned how it is proven that the animal itself is the catalyst for change. Scientific American (Lilienfeldand Arkowitz(2008) published an article entitled "Can Animals Aid Therapy?" where, although they admit to many benefits in using an animal as an adjunct to therapy, they question the long term effects of its use. And in an article published in "eSkeptic", the newsletter of the Skeptic Society at the California Institute of Technology in Pasadena, criticizing Animal Assisted Therapy ("Zootherapy Debunked," Feb. 2012), Charles Danten labeled the early research published on Animal Assisted Therapy as "pseudoscience," and said that most of the early research was merely simple anecdotal observations rather than scientific experiments. He explains that there are two types of studies: 1. Descriptive or hypothesis-generating studies and 2. Studies designed to test a hypothesis (where the assumption is that the hypothesis is false), and he points out that most (if not all) of the research published on Animal Assisted Therapy is the first type.

SHOULD YOU CONSIDER ANIMAL ASSISTED THERAPY

Unfortunately there is limited scientific research on the actual benefits of using an animal in mental health settings. Due to this, it is difficult to judge if using an animal in a mental health setting represents the best, or beneficial choice. Children and adults who have not been treated kindly tend to be less gentle with animals (Mallon, 1994). Since this population may be more likely to seek treatment, your animal may be at higher risk of harm. Therapist needs to be able to step in and take appropriate steps to ensure client and animal safety. The therapist must be able to facilitate client/animal interactions in the pursuit of therapeutic gains. Some of the ways they can do this are:

- Teaching about the humane treatment of animals
- Using client/animal interactions as teachable moments
- Teaching respectful and non-violent ways of getting the animal to do what you want it to do
- Helping clients read the animal's non-verbal cues
- Helping change behavior and meet therapeutic goals
- Modeling the way we interact with our animal as a metaphor for the therapeutic relationship

LEGAL CONSIDERATIONS

When I consider the legal ramifications of using an animal in the psychotherapy process, I think not only of laws regarding this but also how I might have to justify the inclusion of an animal should I ever have to have to go to court on behalf of a client. These are some (but not all) of the things to consider when bringing an animal into the psychotherapy room:

- Inclusion of the animal should *always* be voluntary, and a release should be signed by the client (or the parent or guardian if the client is a child) to include the animal. The clients should always reserve the right to opt out at any time. If the client is a child and the parent has agreed to the use of the animal, the animal should be removed at once if the child is afraid of or uncomfortable with the presence of the animal.

- In my practice I have clients (or their parents if they are a child) sign a "Hold Harmless Agreement" which outlines what I have done to consider their or their child's safety in working with the animal. I also warn them that there are no guarantees when working with a live animal. Even so, there is always a risk that someone could sue you for damages if, for instance, the client is harmed by the animal.

- Does your lease allow you to have an animal on the premises (other than an assistance animal)? If not, you will need to add this to your lease.

- Does your office complex, agency or school allow animals? Never bring an animal to an agency or a school without written permission from those in charge.

- Does your general liability insurance cover your animal at work? Does your homeowners insurance? A colleague of mine recently was able to get her homeowners insurance to add a special rider to her policy covering her dog at work, but I was recently denied the same option when I called and requested the same thing (and we have the same provider!) I'm looking into this further, but be sure to look into who might insure your animal in case of an incident.

- Your client should never be left alone unsupervised with the animal (especially a child) to minimize the risk of an unforeseen incident.

- There is always the risk of physical harm to the client (allergies, being bitten, knocked down, exposed to parasites, bacteria or disease, etc.)

ETHICAL CONSIDERATIONS

There are several ethical issues to consider when bringing an animal into your practice. Some are:

- Therapist must practice within their scope of expertise, therefore the therapist and the animal must have specialized training to do this type of work.

- Ethically we owe it to our clients to provide the best care available. Koganet, et al. (1999) wrote that "It is not ethical to use only Animal Assisted Therapy and to exclude other treatments that have been proven successful. At this time it seems evident that Animal Assisted Therapy should be used as a supplement to other proven methods"

- I believe it is unethical for an untrained handler to take an untrained/untested animal into their psychotherapy practice. This could put them, their clients, and the animal at risk. Therapists should seek out training in Animal Assisted Therapy, and the animals should be obedience trained and tested by a credible screening agent for its appropriateness for use in this capacity.

- Possible emotional harm can be done to the client (such as if the client bonds to the animal and it dies). Also, what if a client has had a traumatic experience with an animal in the past?

PRACTICAL CONSIDERATIONS

Here are some practical things to consider:

- You must have knowledge of animal behavior and body language to ensure the emotional well being of the animal.

- You must attend to the animals needs during and between sessions (food, water, sleep, elimination).

- You need to be sure the office complex allows dogs on the premises, and you must clean up after your animal.

- You may need to arrange for care for your animal (especially a dog) if you need to leave the office for a meeting, etc.

- You should consider what would happen if your animal barks or makes noise during or between sessions. Could this be disruptive to others?

- You must have a way of remembering which clients do or don't have signed permission to work with your animal so you don't accidently expose a client to the animal (I put "NO DOG" next to that client's name in my calendar).

- The animal needs a safe, comfortable place to rest outside of the room when not used in session.

- It's imperative that you disclose to clients (preferably before intake) that there is an animal in your office. Some people are very sensitive or allergic to animals or very fearful of animals due to traumatic experiences from the past. The presence of the animal (even if it is not in the same room) might make them ill, anxious, or panic stricken. They may choose to use another therapist if this is a significant issue for them. It's important that you resist the urge to help people get over their fear of animals if it's your goal and not the client's. The client drives the therapy process.

- You must have heightened sensitivity to aggressive, naughty, or inappropriate behavior by your animal. No excuses. If you animal exhibits any of these behaviors you should either hire a trainer to help extinguish the behavior before further exposure to your clients or retire your animal. Our number one priority is our client's safety.

"Emotional healing is a most amazing gift
that's bestowed by our furry friends.."

Chelle Thompson

CHOOSING AN ANIMAL

If you decide to include an animal in your practice, it is of the utmost importance to chose an animal that is suited for the demands of this type of work. Like they say in real estate, the three most important factors are location, location, and location. Similarly, the three most important factors in choosing a therapy animal are temperament, temperament, and temperament. Your animal should be easy going, comfortable around people, tolerant of handling, and neutral towards other animals.

Some animals to avoid are those that have a history of aggression, have health problems, are sensitive to touch or sound, have a history of trauma, are unpredictable, are food aggressive, are overly rambunctious, shed profusely, or are difficult to control (among others). Don't be tempted to use your family dog in your practice because it would be fun or convenient to have them at work. This could prove to be very dangerous for your clients and your dog. Be sure that they have the correct temperament, training and have been screened and tested by an outside professional.

PREPARING YOUR ANIMAL AND YOURSELF

Once you have chosen an appropriate animal, it is important that you get trained in Animal Assisted Therapy and that your dog has obedience training as well as successful completion of a therapy dog screening exam. The training you receive in Animal Assisted Therapy should help you understand how to read your animal's body language (especially for signs of stress) and learn appropriate expectations for your animal on the job.

Therapy dog screening examinations are offered by several therapy dog organizations (such as Pet Partners, Animal Health Foundation, Caring Creatures, Therapy Dogs International, and Therapy Dogs United, Inc., to name a few). Many are primarily testing for animals to perform Animal Assisted Activities, but the test appears rigorous enough to be suitable for a therapy office. It's even better if you can find one that tests specifically for psychotherapy. Be sure you have an in-person screening for your animal - not just a form you complete online. I believe we all need a second set of eyes on our animals because we can easily be blinded by love to their inappropriate behaviors. Once they are certified, our animal should be rescreened on a regular basis.

"To err is human, to forgive, canine."

Anonymous

CASE STUDIES

The following are several examples of how Scamp has worked with clients in my practice:

(Note: Some details have been changed to protect my clients' identities)

An 11 year old girl came for an intake session who's father had recently been killed in an automobile accident. When I opened the door I saw her sitting on a chair with her arms folded, looking down, and appearing scared and angry. When I invited her and her mother to come into my office, she didn't budge from her position. Her mother gently coaxed her, and seeing no way out she finally rose from her chair and followed her mother into my office. The girl continued to look down, and I noticed she was fighting back tears. Before I sat down, I asked her if she liked dogs. She looked up to me for the first time and said, "Real dogs? Yes!" I summoned Scamp from the adjacent room, and he knew just what to do. He bounded into the room and nearly flew into this child's lap, covering her with kisses. She spent the entire session smiling and cuddling the dog, and at the end she hugged Scamp and told him she couldn't wait to see him again. As if by magic, the rapport that would have taken several sessions to establish was already there.

2. I had been seeing a 17 year old boy who was very
    angry - particularly toward his mother. One session,
    while his mother waited in the waiting room, the boy
    told me hated his mother and he was planning to kill
    himself when he got home from his session. I asked
    how he planned to do it, and he shared his plan with
    me. I could tell he was serious, so I was forced to call
    the authorities to take him to a place where he could
    be safe. He was not aware that the authorities were on
    their way (or he might have bolted from my office), so
    we sat and talked about other things until the officers
    arrived.

    Somehow Scamp sensed that this young man was in
    trouble, and he refused to get off of the boy's lap. The
    boy was gentle with Scamp, and petting him appeared
    to have a calming effect on him. When the authorities
    arrived, Scamp remained on the boy's lap. The officer
    used the presence of Scamp to bond with the boy. He
    asked him questions such as "Do you have a dog at
    home?" and "Do you like dogs?" The officer also
    shared stories about his own dog to bond with the
    boy. Soon the boy was calm enough to go with the
    officer. Scamp jumped off his lap.

3. A 3 year old who had been molested by her grandfather loved to play with the dollhouse, and she often used the doll house figures to represent people in her own family. She rarely played directly with Scamp, so he usually slept in a chair in the playroom during her sessions. Often she would use the figures to recreate the traumatic experiences involving her grandfather, which at times proved to be overwhelming for her. Whenever she became overwhelmed in her play she would run over to Scamp, give him a hug, and run back to the dollhouse to continue her play.

It appeared to me that she used the dog to ground herself so she could continue processing her trauma. Things were very different in her therapy process when Scamp was not there. She would wander around the room having trouble deciding what to do. She seemed lost. The presence of Scamp seemed so important to her that I made sure Scamp was present for her until she was finished with her treatment.

4. I was working with a 10 year old girl who struggled with poor social skills. She was very creative and loved to sew, so nearly every session she would sew some creation out of felt. She would choose her felt pieces and lay them out on the floor while she planned her project. For some reason, as soon as she laid out her felt Scamp would run over and lay down on it, turn over onto his back, and just stare at her (which is a behavior he never did with any other child).

At first she would get frustrated and try to force Scamp off of the felt, but Scamp would simply ignore her or get up, circle around, and then lay back down on the felt again. Eventually she tried using other, more collaborative strategies to get Scamp to move which proved more successful. We were able to correlate the aggressive strategies she was using at school to get other kids to play with her with the forceful strategies she was using with Scamp. She started using more appropriate ways to engage her friends at school with great results.

FINAL CONSIDERATIONS

Working with my therapy dog for the last ten years has had its rewards. Some of the ways my dog has helped in my practice are:

- Bringing reluctant children into therapy
- Helping reduce anxiety and establish rapport quickly
- Making the therapy process more human for a child
- Modeling acceptance and compassion for the child
- Comforting the child when the child is overwhelmed
- Children are not tempted to hug me –they hug the dog instead

Some of the ways the children I see have utilized the dog are:

- Feeding him by hand
- Drawing pictures for him and of him
- Making things for him
- Confiding in him
- Using him as an emotional anchor during difficult play
- Comparing their issues with the dog's (yes, he's got issues!)
- Watching how the therapist accepts the dog's issues as a model for how she might accept theirs
- Including the dog directly in their play (he can often be found starring in his own puppet show)

"I think dogs are the most amazing creatures; they give unconditional love. For me they are the role model for being alive"

Gilda Radnor

REFERENCES & SUGGESTED READING

Barker, S.B., & Dawson, K.S. (1998). The effects of animal-assisted therapy on anxiety ratings of hospitalized psychiatric patients. Psychiatric Services, 49, 797-801

Chandler, C.K., Portrie-Bethke, T.L., Barrio Minton, C.A., Fernando, D.M., O'Callaghan, D.M., (2010). Matching Animal-Assisted Therapy Techniques and Intentions with Counseling Guiding Theories. Journal of Mental Health Counseling, 32 (4), 354-374.

Jasperson, R A. (2010). Animal-Assisted Therapy with Female Inmates with Mental Illness: A Case Example From a Pilot Program. Journal of Offender Rehabilitation, 49, 417–433.

Kogan, L.R., Granger, B.P., Fitchett, J.A., Helmer, K.A. & Young, K.J. (1999). The human team approach for children with emotional disorders: Two case studies. Child & Youth Care Forum, 28, 105-121

Kovacs, Z., Kis, R., Rozsa, S., Rozsa, L., (2004). Animal-assisted therapy for middle-aged schizophrenic patients living in a social institution. A pilot study. <u>Clinical Rehabilitation</u>, <u>18</u>, 483-486.

Lange, A.M., Cox, J.A., Bernert, D.A., Jenkins, C.D. (2006/2007). Is Counseling Going to the Dogs? An Exploratory Study Related to the Inclusion of an Animal in Group Counseling with Adolescents. <u>Journal of Creativity in Mental Health</u>, <u>2</u> (2), 17-31.

Lilienfeld, S.O., Arkowitz, H,. (2008). Can Animals Aid Therapy?. <u>Scientific American Mind</u>, 19(3).

Mallon, G.P. (1994). Cow as co-therapist: Utilization of farm animals as therapeutic aids with children in residential treatment. <u>Child and Adolescent Social Work Journal</u>, 11. 455-474

Minatrea, N.B., Wesley, M.C. (2008). Reality Therapy Goes to the Dogs. <u>International Journal of Reality Therapy</u>, <u>28(1)</u>, 69-77.

Parshall, D.P. (2003). Research and Reflection: Animal Assisted Therapy in Mental Health Settings. <u>Counseling and Values</u>, <u>48</u>, 47-56.

Pichot, T., Coulter, M. (2009). Book Review: *Animal-Assisted Brief Therapy—A Solution-Focused Approach*, <u>Social Work in Health Care</u>, <u>48</u>, 815-816.

Prothmann, A., Bienert, M., & Ettrich, C. (2006). Dogs in child psychotherapy: Effects on State of Mind, <u>Anthrozoos</u>, <u>19</u>, 265-277

Reichert, E. (1994). Play And Animal-Assisted Therapy: For Sexually Abused Girls Ages 9-13. <u>Family Therapy</u>, <u>21</u> (1), 55-62.

Ravn, K., (2011), Therapy dogs make the rounds in more healthcare settings, <u>Los Angeles Times</u>, July 18, 2011, Health Section

Serpell, J.A. (2000). Animal companions and human well-being: An historical exploration of the value of human-animal relationships. In A. Fine (Ed.), <u>Animal Assisted Therapy</u> (pp. 3-18). San Diego, CA: Academic Press.

Sockalingam, S, Li, M, Krishnadev, U. Hanson, K. Balaban, K, Pacione, L.R., Bhalerao, S, (2008). Use of Animal-Assisted Therapy in The Rehabilitation Of An Assault Victim With A

Concurrent Mood Disorder. <u>Issues in Mental Health Nursing</u>, 29, 73-84.

VanFleet, R. (2008). *Play Therapy with Kids & Canines: Benefits for Children's Developmental and Psychosocial Health.* Professional Resourse Press.

Walsh, F. (2009). Human-Animal Bonds II: The Role of Pets in Family Systems and Family Therapy. <u>Family Process</u>. <u>48</u>, (4), 481-499.

Special thanks to Pet Partners/Delta Society for providing much of the information on Animal Assisted Therapy

ABOUT THE THERAPY DOG

Ten years ago I contacted an animal rescue group and explained that I was looking for a dog who had an excellent rapport with children to add to my therapy practice. They matched me with "Scamp", a then-two year old terrier mix who had been days away from being euthanized at a local shelter. In the last ten years Scamp has helped change the lives of hundreds of children struggling with behavioral and/or emotional challenges. I can't thank him enough for his kindness, dedication, thousands of "doggie kisses" along the way.

ABOUT THE AUTHOR

Susan Kelsey is a licensed Marriage and Family Therapist and Registered Play Therapist-Supervisor in private practice in Orange County, California. Susan's practice is limited to children of all ages - from toddlers through teens. Susan specializes in the use of play therapy and Animal Assisted Therapy to help children work through their challenges.

Susan is a nationally recognized speaker and presenter on subjects related to the quality treatment of children and adolescents. Susan has been featured in numerous parenting magazines as an expert on issues relating to children, and was interviewed on the television news show, "Daybreak OC".

For additional information about Susan and her practice, please visit www.susankelseymft.com